The Particle Model of Matter

Roberta Baxter

Raintree

www.raintreepublishers.co.uk
Visit our website to find out more information about Raintree books.

To order:
☎ Phone 44 (0) 1865 888112
📄 Send a fax to 44 (0) 1865 314091
💻 Visit the Raintree Bookshop at www.raintreepublishers.co.uk to browse our catalogue and order online.

Edited by Megan Cotugno and Andrew Farrow
Designed by Philippa Jenkins
Original illustrations ©Pearson Education Ltd
Illustrated by KJA-artists.com
Picture research by Ruth Blair
Originated by Modern Age
Printed and bound in China by Leo Paper Group

ISBN 978 1 406210 78 1
13 12 11 10 09
10 9 8 7 6 5 4 3 2 1

British Library Cataloguing in Publication Data
A full catalogue record for this book is available from the British Library.

Acknowledgements
We would like to thank the following for allowing their pictures to be reproduced in this publication: © Action Plus/Neil Tingle p. **4**; © Alamy/AM Corporation p. **32**; © Alamy/Charles Stirling (Diving) p. **30**; © Alamy/G. P. Bowater p. **34**; © Alamy/ImageState pp. **iii** (Contents, top), **26**; © Alamy/Phototake Inc. p. **35**; © Alamy/The Photolibrary Wales p. **38**; © Corbis p. **5**; © Corbis/Schultheiss Productions/Zefa p. **29**; © iStockphoto p. **37**; © Pearson Education Ltd/Gareth Boden p. **24**; © Pearson Education Ltd/Trevor Clifford p. **33**; © PhotoDisc/StockTrek p. **6**; © Science & Society Picture Library pp. **10**, **14**; © Science Photo Library/Charles D. Winters p. **8**; © Science Photo Library/Drs. A Yazdani & D. J. Hornbaker p. **7**; © Science Photo Library/Health Protection Agency p. **25**; © Science Photo Library/John Heseltine p. **18**; © Science Photo Library/John Sanford p. **31**; © Science Photo Library/Lawrence Lawry pp. **iii** (Contents, bottom), **9**; © Science Photo Library/Omikron p. **12**; © Science Photo Library/Philippe Psaila p. **40**; © Science Photo Library/Tex Kinsman p. **36**; © Shutterstock p. **22**, background images and design features throughout.

Cover photographs reproduced with permission of © Science Photo Library/Mike Agliolo **main**; © Science Photo Library/Steve Allen **inset**.

The publishers would like to thank literacy consultant Nancy Harris and content consultant Dr. Ted Dolter for their assistance in the preparation of this book.

Every effort has been made to contact copyright holders of any material reproduced in this book. Any omissions will be rectified in subsequent printings if notice is given to the publishers.

Some words are shown in bold, **like this**. These words are explained in the glossary. You will find important information and definitions underlined, <u>like this</u>.

Contents

What metal is actually a liquid at room temperature? Find out on page 26.

Diamonds are made up of atoms of what element? Find out on page 9!

Matter

Everything around us is made up of **matter**. Rocks, metal bridge parts, skin, and water are all matter. Even things we cannot see, like the air around us, are made of matter.

What is matter?

But what is matter? What is it made of? Can it change? You will find out in this book.

Everything in the universe is made of matter. Matter has **mass** (what we sometimes call weight) and takes up space. Matter is made of tiny particles, or parts, that cannot be seen. The matter of air is very different from rock or milk. But it is still matter.

This lifter can certainly tell that matter has mass!

Forms of matter

Matter comes in many forms. It can be solid, liquid, or gas. Think about water. It can be solid ice, or the liquid water we drink, or a gas, like steam. But all the kinds of water are matter.

What is matter made of?
Find out on the next pages…

Everything we see around us is matter in some form.

How much do we know about matter?

We know a lot about matter, but are still learning about it all the time. Scientists are studying matter and how it acts. They are learning about the tiny particles that make up matter. Learning about matter helps scientists understand the world around them. It helps chemists to create new chemicals, such as medicines, **synthetic fuels**, and new building materials.

Atoms and elements

Matter is made up of tiny particles called atoms. Atoms are so tiny that they cannot be seen even with the most powerful light microscope. About 20 trillion hydrogen atoms could fit into the full stop at the end of this sentence.

What is an atom like?

To know what an atom is like, imagine a person cutting a piece of copper wire. What is the result? The result is two smaller pieces of wire. If a smaller piece is cut again and again, what happens? The pieces get smaller and smaller.

Is it still copper? Yes, even when it is down to the size of an atom. It will be a copper atom, but it cannot be divided any smaller and still be copper.

When a substance is divided down to the smallest particle that is still the same substance, that particle is the atom.

It's difficult to even comprehend the number of atoms that make up the planet Earth.

How do we know?

If scientists cannot easily see atoms, how do they know anything about them? They perform experiments, then they try to think of an idea that would explain the results of those experiments. This idea is called a model. By learning about atoms, scientists can predict what atoms will do.

Scientists used a special instrument called a scanning tunnelling microscope to get the closest picture of atoms ever seen. In a picture from this machine, a person can see the humps and balls that are the atoms.

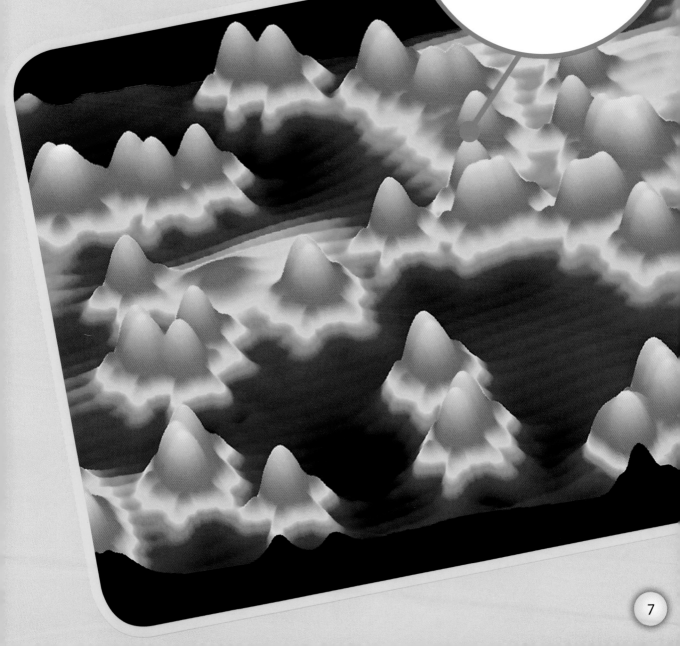

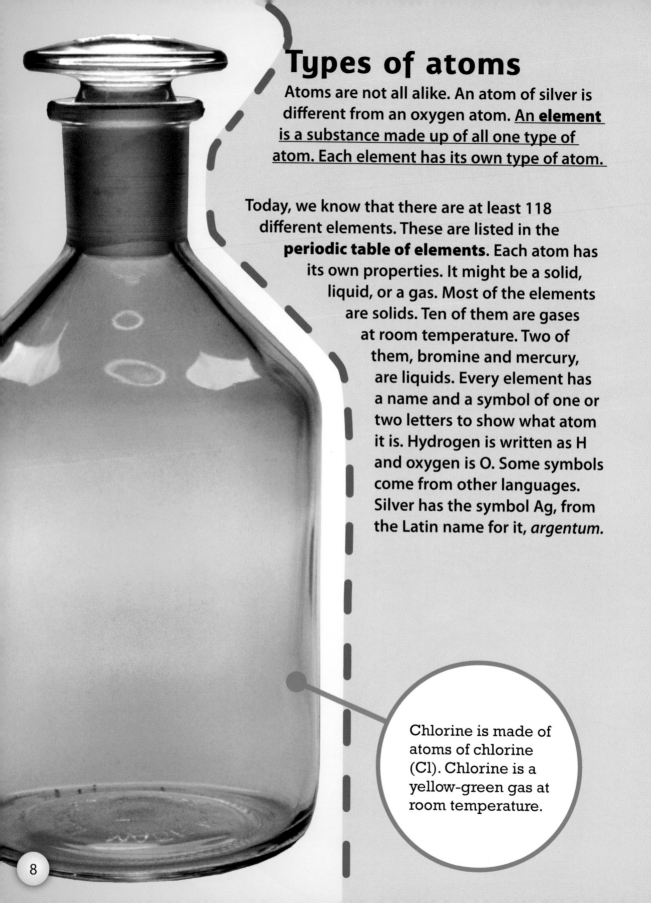

Types of atoms

Atoms are not all alike. An atom of silver is different from an oxygen atom. <u>An **element** is a substance made up of all one type of atom. Each element has its own type of atom.</u>

Today, we know that there are at least 118 different elements. These are listed in the **periodic table of elements**. Each atom has its own properties. It might be a solid, liquid, or a gas. Most of the elements are solids. Ten of them are gases at room temperature. Two of them, bromine and mercury, are liquids. Every element has a name and a symbol of one or two letters to show what atom it is. Hydrogen is written as H and oxygen is O. Some symbols come from other languages. Silver has the symbol Ag, from the Latin name for it, *argentum*.

Chlorine is made of atoms of chlorine (Cl). Chlorine is a yellow-green gas at room temperature.

Old ideas about elements

The ancient Greeks decided that everything was made from four elements – fire, water, earth, and air. They believed that all matter was made from these four elements combined together. They thought that a log contained all four elements. When a log burns, they thought fire and air are released, water seeps out, and earth is left behind. The water that seeps out is really sap from the tree and the earth is the ashes that remain.

Scientists went along with the idea of four elements for a long time. Then, in the 1800s, people discovered that there were many elements. Each element had its own atom.

Diamonds are made up of atoms of carbon. Carbon is a solid at room temperature. Diamonds are a very hard solid.

Atomic structure

It took years for modern ideas about **atoms** to develop. One of the most important scientists was John Dalton, an English chemist. He said that atoms were like tiny, hard balls connected to each other.

Dalton's Ideas

In 1807 Dalton said that everything is made of atoms, like iron or sodium. He also said that there were many different kinds of atoms. When different kinds of atoms combined or reacted together, they formed new substances.

Dalton said that atoms are not destroyed when they combine with other atoms to make new substances. He said a sodium atom is the same whether it is in sodium metal or is combined with a chlorine atom to make sodium chloride, table salt. A **chemical reaction** or change will not change an **element** into another type of atom.

John Dalton made a model of matter from round wooden balls connected with sticks.

Atoms have parts

Once chemists agreed that there were many kinds of atoms, they began to think about what they looked like. At the end of the 1800s, another Englishman, J. J. Thomson, discovered that atoms are not solid balls. He found a tiny particle that was part of every kind of atom. It is called an **electron**. Electrons are particles with a negative charge (-).

Protons

Then the **proton** was discovered. Protons have a positive charge (+). Every kind of atom has a different number of protons. The number of protons in an atom tells us what kind of atom it is. A carbon atom has six protons. There are 29 protons in a copper atom and 20 in a calcium atom.

If one proton could be added to the six in a carbon atom, it would be like a nitrogen atom, which has seven.

Carbon has six protons, shown on the left. Add one and you would have a nitrogen nucleus, as shown on the right.

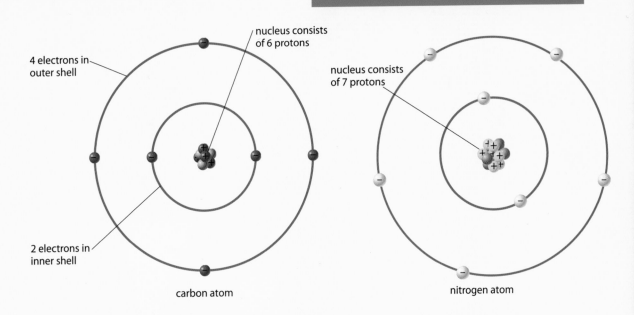

4 electrons in outer shell

nucleus consists of 6 protons

2 electrons in inner shell

carbon atom

nucleus consists of 7 protons

nitrogen atom

Ideas about the atom

Scientists wondered how these particles fit together in an atom. J. J. Thomson thought the atom was like plum pudding. He said the electrons were scattered throughout the atom like plums in plum pudding.

Rutherford's experiment

Ernest Rutherford, a scientist from New Zealand, did some experiments with a very thin piece of gold foil. He used a special machine to shoot some heavy atomic particles at the gold. Most of the particles went right through. But some of them bounced back. Rutherford wondered why.

Rutherford was very surprised at his discovery. It was like a person firing a cannon shell at a piece of tissue paper and the shell bouncing back.

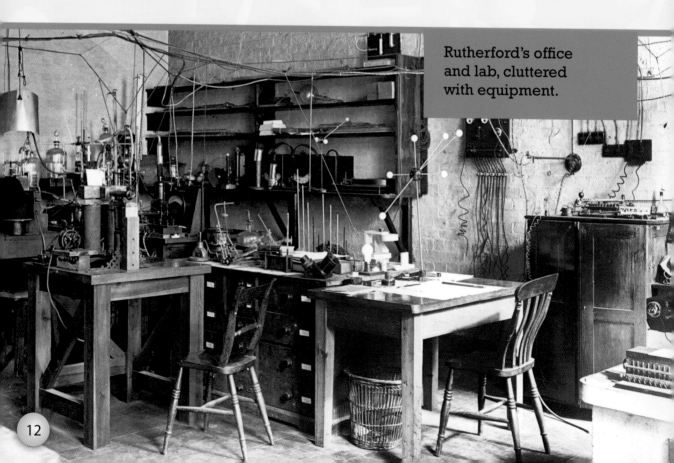

Rutherford's office and lab, cluttered with equipment.

Why did the particles bounce back?

Rutherford decided that his particles were deflected by something in the middle of the atoms. He called it the **nucleus**. Rutherford created a model of the atom with a heavy, positively charged nucleus in the centre and the negatively charged electrons circling it. He concluded that the rest of the atom was like empty space.

What was the explanation?

Imagine a person kicking a football towards a pole. There could be several different results. Many kicks would go right past the pole. Some might hit just the edge of the pole and bounce a little bit sideways. A few could hit the pole squarely and bounce back at the kicker.

In Rutherford's experiment, many of the particles pass through the empty space of the gold atoms, while some particles are deflected away by the heavy nucleus.

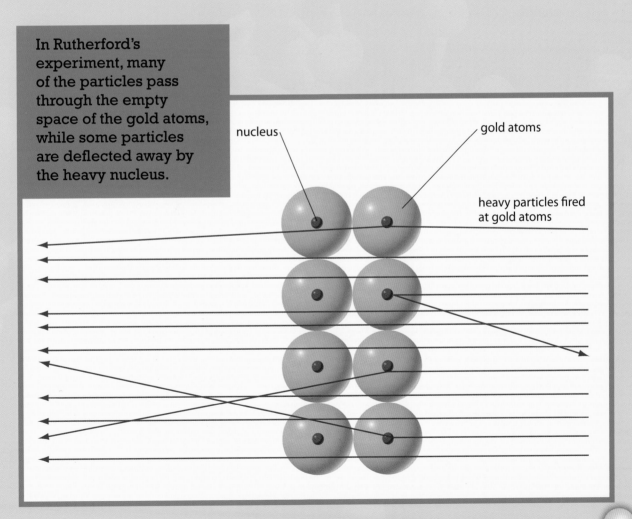

nucleus

gold atoms

heavy particles fired at gold atoms

Better ideas about atoms

There was a problem with Rutherford's idea, or model, about atoms. Surely, the negative electrons would be attracted to the positive nucleus. The atom would then collapse!

Niels Bohr's ideas

A scientist from Denmark, Niels Bohr, explained why this would not happen. He developed a model of the atom that looks like a solar system. He too showed that the electrons circled around the nucleus. Bohr explained that electrons don't collapse into the nucleus because they have a certain amount of **energy**. They **orbit** in special energy levels. This keeps the electrons from moving toward the nucleus. For an electron to jump to a higher energy level, it must get extra energy. If it falls back to a lower energy level, energy is released.

Bohr's model is similar to planets in orbit around a star in a solar system.

Neutrons

In 1932 another particle was found in atoms. A British scientist, James Chadwick, found a particle he called the **neutron**. A neutron is neutral; it has no charge. The neutrons of an atom are in the nucleus, along with the protons.

Hydrogen is the only atom without a neutron. A neutron is neutral: it has no charge. The nucleus of an oxygen atom contains protons and neutrons.

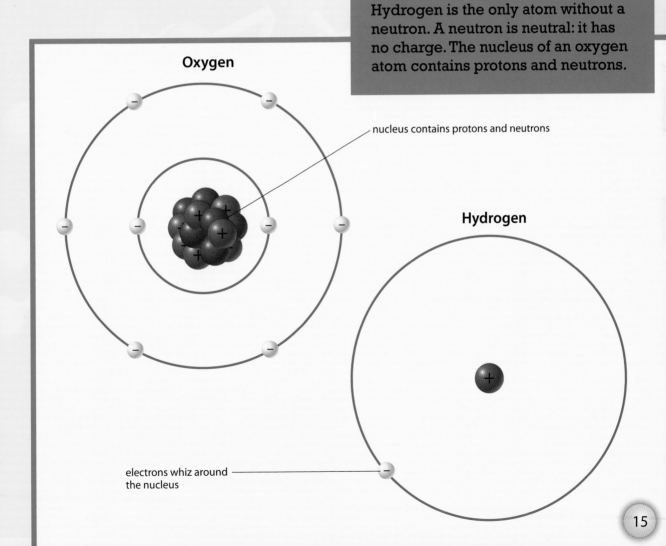

Oxygen

nucleus contains protons and neutrons

Hydrogen

electrons whiz around the nucleus

Structure makes a difference

All **atoms** have **protons** and **neutrons** tightly packed into a **nucleus** and **electrons** circling around. Atoms of different **elements** have a different number of protons. <u>Each atom of an element has an equal number of protons and electrons.</u>

Amazing carbon

But there is more to the structure of elements. The element carbon comes in three very different forms. The soot from a candle is made of carbon. Soot is made from layers of atoms. The same structure is found in graphite, a type of carbon used in pencil leads and as a **lubricant**. The carbon atoms are in the shape of hexagons (six-sided shapes) linked to one another in a layer. Each carbon atom is linked tightly to three more carbons, but the layers are only loosely linked. They easily slide past each other, giving a slippery texture. The graphite in pencil lead allows pieces of carbon to flake off and make marks on the paper. Because graphite is slippery, it can be used as a lubricant, to loosen things.

Diamonds are carbon, too

Another structure of carbon is found in diamonds. Each carbon atom is attached to four other carbon atoms with tight bonds. This time, the structure is rigid. This means diamonds are very hard. Diamonds are used in jewellery and to make cutting tools. Diamonds are so hard that they can cut other hard materials, including steel and other diamonds.

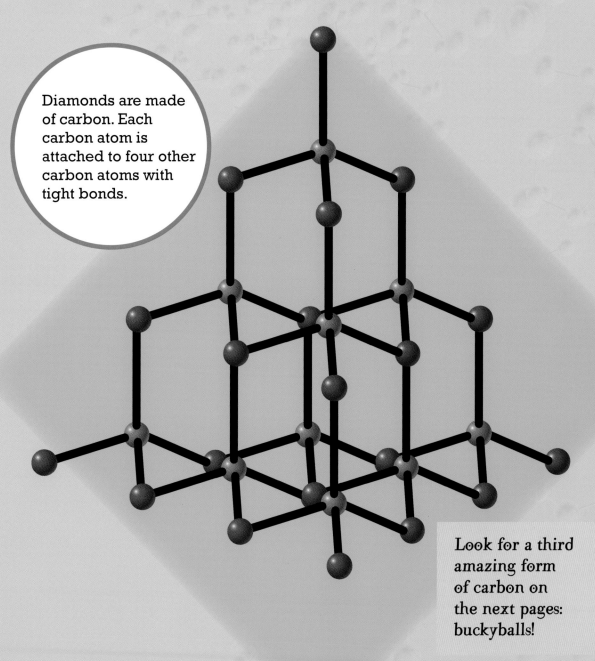

Diamonds are made of carbon. Each carbon atom is attached to four other carbon atoms with tight bonds.

Look for a third amazing form of carbon on the next pages: buckyballs!

Buckyballs

Since 1985 scientists have discovered and studied a new structure of carbon. It is called a buckyball.

Why is it called a buckyball?

Sixty carbon atoms form a **molecule** in the shape of a football. The molecule looks like the pattern of a geodesic dome (see photo below). A geodesic dome shape is very strong. It was used in buildings designed by an American named Buckminster Fuller, so scientists named the new molecule "buckminsterfullerene", or buckyball for short.

The geodesic dome has been used in human architecture because of the strong properties of its shape.

The structure of a buckyball

The buckyball molecule (right) looks like a ball with a hollow centre. The 60 carbons are arranged in a pattern of 12 pentagons (5-sided shapes) and 20 hexagons (6-sided shapes). The molecule can be compressed and then springs back to its original shape. It is very strong, like a geodesic dome. The molecule can hit metal surfaces at 32,000 kilometres per hour (20,000 miles per hour) and bounce off intact. Other molecules would be destroyed at that speed.

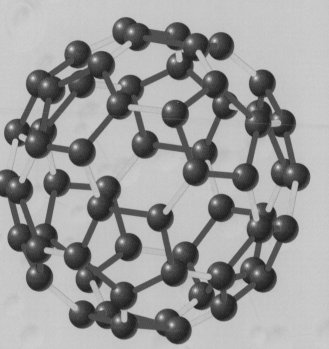

Using buckyballs

Scientists are searching for ways to use the buckyball.

• One idea is putting medicine in its centre. The buckyball would carry the medicine directly to the cells that need it without affecting other cells.

• Buckyballs might be used as molecular sponges to soak up pollutants.

• Computer chips built with buckyballs would be faster than computer chips today.

Atoms combine

Atoms can combine with each other. When they do this they form **molecules** and **compounds**. <u>Compounds contain atoms of two or more elements</u> held together by chemical bonds. <u>Molecules are the smallest units formed when atoms combine with each other.</u> But how do atoms combine and form these bonds?

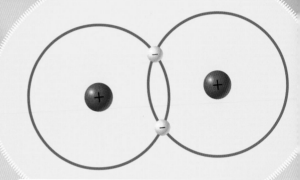

Hydrogen gas is a molecule made up of two hydrogen atoms. The hydrogen atoms (H) share their electrons with each other. Scientists write this as H_2.

Sharing electrons

Sometimes the **electrons** circling the **nucleus** of one atom are shared with electrons from another atom. This forms a bond that is like children holding hands. For example, two hydrogen atoms bond to an oxygen atom and make a molecule of water. The electrons from the hydrogen atoms (H) are shared with the electrons from the oxygen atom (O). These bonds hold the water molecule together. Scientists write the water molecule as H_2O.

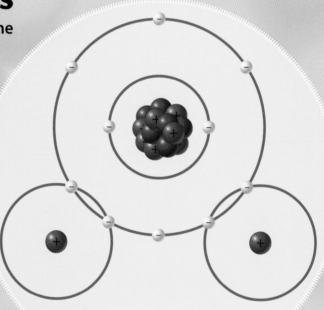

A molecule of water contains two atoms of hydrogen and one atom of oxygen.

Giving and taking atoms

Sometimes atoms give up electrons to form bonds with other atoms. The other atoms take these extra electrons. For example, a sodium atom (Na) releases one electron to a chlorine atom (Cl) to make a molecule of sodium chloride. Scientists write this is NaCl. Sodium chloride is the chemical we call salt.

sodium + chlorine → sodium chloride

Na + Cl → NaCl

When a salt molecule, NaCl, is formed, the sodium atom releases one electron to the chlorine atom. This sharing of electrons often forms a strong bond, as illustrated below right.

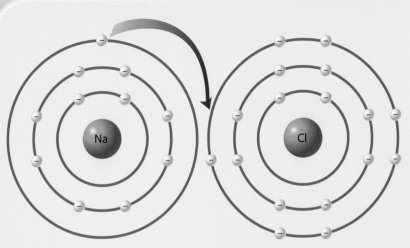

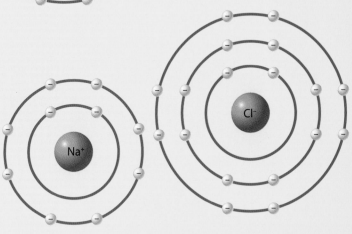

Chemical reactions

A chemical reaction happens when atoms of one element combine with atoms of another element.

There are several signs that can show that a **chemical change** has happened.

- The **products** are different from the beginning chemicals.
- Sometimes heat and light are produced.
- Sometimes the chemicals get colder or warmer.
- Sometimes bubbles of gas are produced.

Different properties

When different kinds of atoms combine into a molecule, the new molecule is different from the atoms. For example, a soft metal called sodium combines with a greenish, poisonous gas named chlorine. The result, or product, is white crystals called sodium chloride. You know sodium chloride as table salt.

Chemical and physical changes

A chemical change is different from a **physical change**. Hydrogen and oxygen combining into water is a chemical change.

In a physical change, the matter is the same, but the form changes. Water turning into ice is a physical change.

The combining of atoms to form molecules is also different from a **mixture**. Sand and salt stirred together make a mixture. They do not react into a new molecule.

Think about this!

Which of these things show a chemical change and which show a physical change?

1. Water heated in a kettle, producing steam

2. Logs burning in a campfire

3. Copper metal melting in a furnace

4. Bicarbonate of soda added to vinegar, producing bubbles

5. Alcohol evaporating

6. A lightstick glowing

Answers are below.

Answers
Numbers 1, 3, and 5 are physical changes.
Numbers 2, 4, and 6 are chemical changes.

Changing bonds

In a chemical reaction, molecules switch bonds to form new molecules.
Imagine groups of children holding hands. The children are like atoms in a
molecule. If they swap partners in their group, they have to let go of hands
and take hold of new ones. It is like causing a chemical reaction to happen.

For example, chemicals called sodium hydroxide and hydrogen chloride react
to form sodium chloride (table salt) and water. You can see how the atoms
switch places to form new molecules.

sodium hydroxide   +   hydrogen chloride $\rightarrow$ sodium chloride +   water

$$NaOH \quad + \quad HCl \quad \rightarrow \quad NaCl \quad + \quad H_2O$$

Does everything react?

Some chemicals react more easily
than others. Neon, the gas found
in neon lights, will not react at all.
Potassium metal is very reactive
with air and water. It must be stored
under oil to keep it from bursting
into flames.

The potassium found in bananas
and other foods is a molecule made
of potassium and other atoms, so it
is not as reactive.

Potassium reacts
violently with water.

Moving electrons

We have seen how electrons are involved in chemical reactions. The electrons in metal atoms are only loosely connected to the atom. The electrons can let go of an atom and move to another one. This flow of electrons through metal is what we call electricity.

Chemical reactions occur when we use a battery. The chemicals in a battery release electrons into a surrounding paste. These electrons have a negative charge and are attracted to positively charged metal rods in the battery. As electrons flow to the metal rods, electricity is produced. We use this electricity to light bulbs, power CD players, or start a car engine.

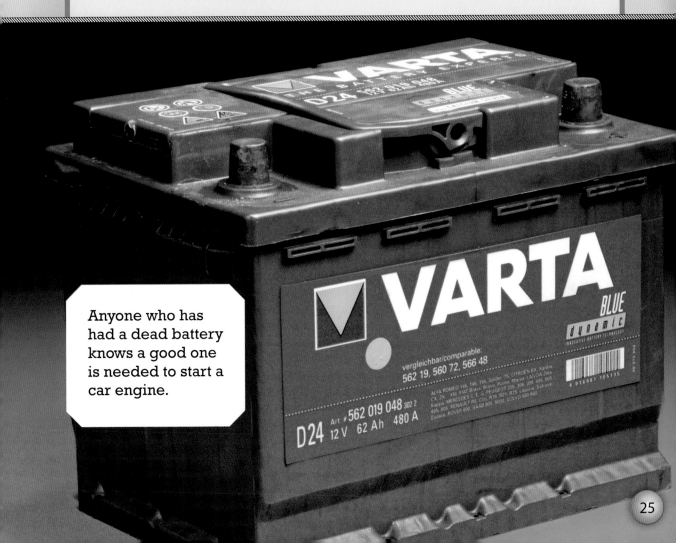

Anyone who has had a dead battery knows a good one is needed to start a car engine.

States of matter

Matter occurs in three states: solid, liquid, and gas.
For example, the three states of water are a liquid, solid
ice, and gaseous water vapor, or steam. Silver is a solid at
room temperature, and hydrogen is a gas. Mercury is a very
unusual metal because it is a liquid at room temperature.

Other substances can also be a solid, liquid, or gas. They can be made to change state, for example from solid to liquid. Matter changes state because of a change in temperature or pressure. To go from one state to another is called a **physical change**. We will look now at how matter can change state from solid to liquid to gas.

The metal mercury is unusual because it is liquid at room temperature.

Solids

In the solid state, the particles of a substance do not have a high amount of **energy**. The particles can still move, but bonds between the **molecules** hold them tightly. They are in close formation to one another, much like people seated in a theatre. The particles are close enough to each other that they cannot be compressed, or squeezed closer together.

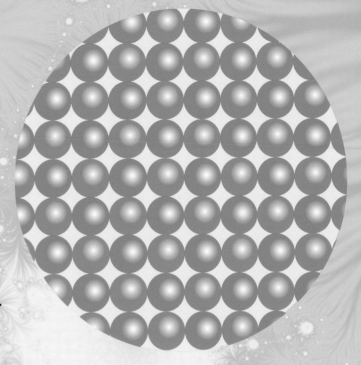

Liquids

When heat or pressure is added to a solid, the particles gain more energy. This breaks some of the bonds between the particles. The particles can move more freely. The solid begins to turn into a liquid. The particles still have some structure as the liquid flows. It is similar to a crowd of people waiting in a line. The particles are still close enough to each other that they cannot be compressed.

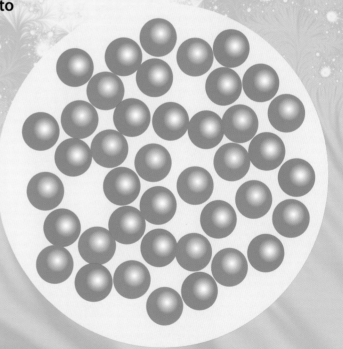

Gases

If more heat or pressure is added to a liquid, the forces between molecules break completely. The particles fly away from each other, and the liquid turns into a gas. Now the particles are flying in every direction. They have none of the structure seen in solids and liquids. They scurry around like people in a busy town.

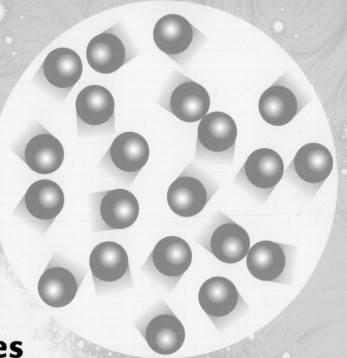

Pressure in gases

Particles in a gas exert pressure because of their rapid movement. They hit anything that gets in their way with lots of tiny forces. For example, air molecules keep bumping into the rubber of a balloon. The tiny forces keep the balloon inflated.

The air around us also has pressure because its **mass** gives it weight. Air pressure pushes down on everything on Earth. There is less air on the top of a mountain than down along the seashore, so at higher altitudes the air pressure decreases.

News Flash: Water can boil at 94° C!

Lower air pressure changes the forces between liquid molecules by pushing down less on the liquid. This means less energy is needed for a liquid to turn into a gas. So the boiling point of any liquid is lower at a higher altitude. In the mountains of Colorado, for example, water boils at about 94° Celsius (202° Fahrenheit) rather than at 100° C (212° F) at sea level!

Water for coffee boils at a lower temperature when camping in the mountains.

Diffusion

The movement of gas particles allows for **diffusion**. Perfume molecules turn from liquid to gas very easily. As they do, they mix into the particles of air. Their movements allow them to spread, or diffuse, through a room.

Try this!

• Place several drops of perfume or vanilla flavouring on a cotton wool ball and leave it on a kitchen counter. Go into the next room and measure how long it takes for the smell to reach you.

• Put a few drops of vanilla flavouring on the inside of a balloon, inflate the balloon and wait. Do you smell vanilla? The vanilla molecules have diffused through the rubber of the balloon.

Changing back

The change of state from solid to liquid and liquid to gas can be reversed. Cooling slows the particles down until they form the loose bonds again. They go from gas to liquid, or liquid to solid. Even gases can be turned to liquids at very cold temperatures or high pressures.

Compressing gases

Gases have large spaces between the particles, so they can be compressed into smaller spaces. A person can squeeze a balloon until it is much smaller because the gas molecules can be forced closer together. If a gas is squeezed enough, it will stop being a gas and turn into a liquid. People cannot squash air enough to liquefy air. But a machine called a compressor can do it.

The air tanks of divers depend on the property of liquid oxygen turning back into a gas at a lower pressure.

Tanks used by divers contain air that has been compressed until it is a liquid. As the diver breathes, the liquid air is pulled from the tank into a device called a regulator. The regulator lowers the pressure on the liquid air. The liquid air turns back into a gas and can be breathed.

This change of state from liquid to gas is also seen in oxygen bottles for people with breathing problems. It is also seen in tanks of liquid gases such as butane and propane, used for heating and cooking.

Plasma

Another state of matter is not found naturally on Earth. It is called plasma. In plasma the electrons have been stripped from gas atoms. The particles of the stripped atoms and the electrons continue to collide with each other, producing light and **energy**. This process is found in fluorescent lights, plasma TV screens, and in stars.

A fourth state of matter, plasma, is found in stars.

Properties of matter

We know that matter takes up space and has **mass**. It also has other properties. One is **density**, or a measure of mass in a certain **volume**. <u>Something that has a lot of mass in a small space is said to have a high density.</u> A tonne of bricks will take up less space than a tonne of water because the bricks are denser.

How dense?

Which is more dense – a rock or a piece of cork of the same size? Why do you think it's the rock? The rock is more dense because it has a lot more mass squeezed into the same amount of volume.

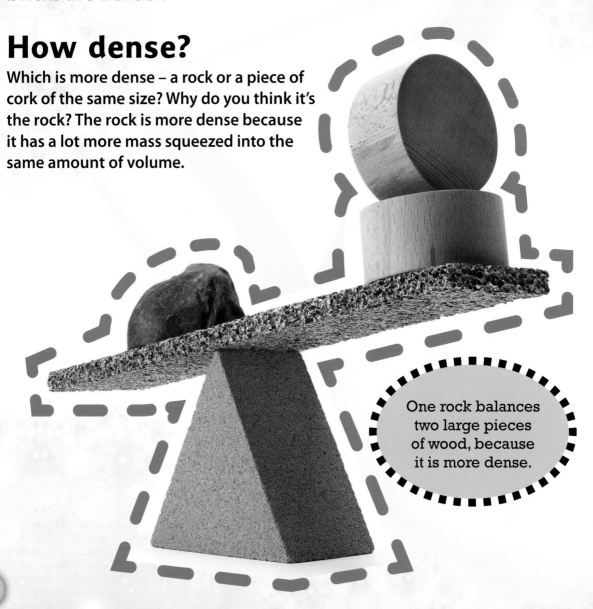

One rock balances two large pieces of wood, because it is more dense.

Buoyancy

Density is related to another property, called **buoyancy**. Items that are less dense (lighter) than water will float. Things that are denser (heavier) than water will sink. So then how do metal ships float? It seems that large ships would not float because their metal would make them heavier than water. However, ships have large sections full of air, so their total density is less than water!

Try this!

Using different densities

Different substances have different densities. Balsa wood, used to make model aeroplanes, is less dense than water, so it floats. Difference in density can cause problems. The chemical oil is also less dense than water. When a ship leaks oil into the ocean, the oil floats on the water. Birds and sea animals get coated with the oil and many then die.

Density can be used to separate mixtures. If two liquids are allowed to layer out in a tube, the lighter substance can be drawn off of the top, leaving the substance that is more dense behind. Try this to find out how:

- Pour about an inch-deep layer of vegetable oil into a clear glass. Then gently pour water on top of the oil.

- Let the mixture stand for a few minutes. What happens and why?

Answer:
The water is more dense than the oil, so the oil floats on top of the water.

Eventually the mixture will separate into layers, due to their different densities.

Boiling point

Another property of matter is **boiling point**. Different liquids boil at different temperatures. For example, rubbing alcohol boils at a lower temperature than water. So a mixture of rubbing alcohol and water can be separated by boiling off the alcohol and leaving the water behind.

Substances will **condense** from a gas back into a liquid at the same temperature as their boiling points.

Using different boiling points

One use of this property is in refining crude oil. Oil is a mixture of many chemicals that have different boiling points, such as gasoline, kerosene, and diesel.

To separate the chemicals, huge columns are built at oil refineries. At the bottom of the column, the crude oil is heated to very high temperatures. The oil turns into a gas and rises up through the column. The temperature decreases up in the column. When the part of the column is the temperature of the boiling point of a particular chemical, that chemical will turn back into liquid. The liquids are collected and saved.

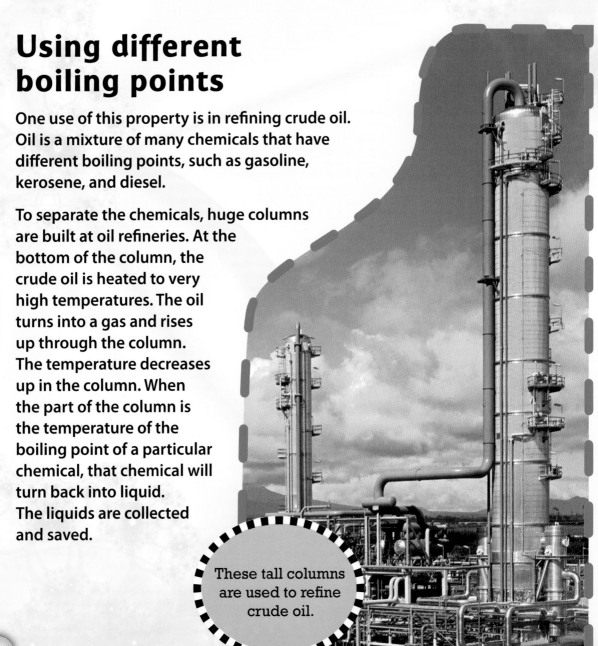

These tall columns are used to refine crude oil.

Identifying liquids

Chemists also use this property of boiling point to identify unknown liquids. If a liquid boils at about 100º C (212º F), it must be water. If it boils at 79º C (174º F), it is alcohol.

Removing pollutants

Boiling can be used to clean salts and other pollutants out of water. For example, if sodium chloride, table salt, is dissolved in water, how can the salt be removed? Boiling the salt water will turn the water into a gas. The gas can be collected in a side tube and cooled back into a liquid. The salt stays in the boiling flask. When the water has boiled out of the first flask, only the solid salt remains. The water that has been collected is pure water with no salt.

Chemists use the property of boiling point to identify liquids.

Amazing water

There is a saying that every snowflake is unique. While it might not be literally true, the structure of water in snowflakes allows a multitude of shapes. Snowflakes form with six sides or legs. The shape of each side varies by the number and position of the water molecules in the snowflake. There are so many possible positions that each snowflake looks different.

Unusual properties

This is just one property of water, which is a very common but unusual chemical.

Most matter becomes denser as it freezes. Water behaves in an opposite way. It becomes less dense. So ice cubes float in a glass of iced tea or soda!

Try this!

Try putting a paper cup full of water in the freezer. Leave it for a few hours. How does it look? The ice will have pushed up out of the cup because it expanded as it froze.

Water may seem common to some of us, but it is certainly a unique substance.

Why is ice unusual?

Why does this happen? Ice is less dense than water because of the structure of the **molecules**. As they freeze, water molecules form a structure with a large amount of open space between the molecules. This means that the molecules are not packed tightly together. Because of the more open space between the molecules, water also expands as it freezes. This makes the ice less dense than water. Other substances shrink as they freeze.

Ice being less dense allows it to float on water, which allows life to survive within lakes like this.

Why floating ice is important

What is the importance of water becoming less dense as it turns into ice? Imagine a fish in a lake. What happens if the ice falls to the bottom of the lake as it freezes?

If ice formed from the bottom of the lake up, fish would be forced to the surface and they would die. Instead, the ice floats on the water because it is less dense. The layer of ice even provides some insulation to keep the water below from freezing. So fish have a safe place to survive through the winter.

New ideas about atoms

The word **atom** means "cannot be divided", but in the 1900s scientists learned that atoms can be split. They found **elements** that have atoms that are unstable. These atoms can split on their own. A famous scientist named Marie Curie studied some of these elements. She named this process of splitting **radioactivity**.

Chain reactions occur over and over in a nuclear power plant.

Using radioactivity

This process is the basis of nuclear power plants. It is also used in nuclear bombs, x-rays, and radioactive materials that are used to treat cancer.

In a nuclear power plant, machines fire streams of **neutrons** at pieces of a radioactive element called uranium 235. When the neutrons hit uranium 235 atoms, the atoms split apart. More neutrons and some energy are released. The extra neutrons hit more uranium and the process continues. More atoms split and more energy is released. The process keeps happening. This is a **chain reaction**.

A subatomic zoo

We know that scientists once believed that atoms were solid balls. Then **electrons**, **protons**, and neutrons were discovered. In recent years, scientists have also discovered particles that make up the protons and neutrons of atoms! So far scientists have found almost 200 subatomic particles. These particles are extremely hard to study because they are hard to detect. They also don't follow the same rules as protons, neutrons, and electrons. They can speed right through even solid material such as lead and steel.

So many smaller particles have been discovered that scientists refer to it as a "subatomic zoo."

Quarks and neutrinos

One particle is called a **quark**. Many people are conducting experiments to learn about quarks and how they work. It seems that three quarks make up a proton or a neutron.

Another extremely tiny particle is associated with the electron. **Neutrinos** are even lighter than electrons and move so fast they can pass through almost anything.

Nanotechnology

Nanotechnology is the field of study about structures a little larger than atoms and **molecules**. That's very small things!

Nanotechnology is named after a unit of measurement called a nanometre. A nanometre is one-billionth of a metre. The head of a pin is 1,000,000 nanometres wide.

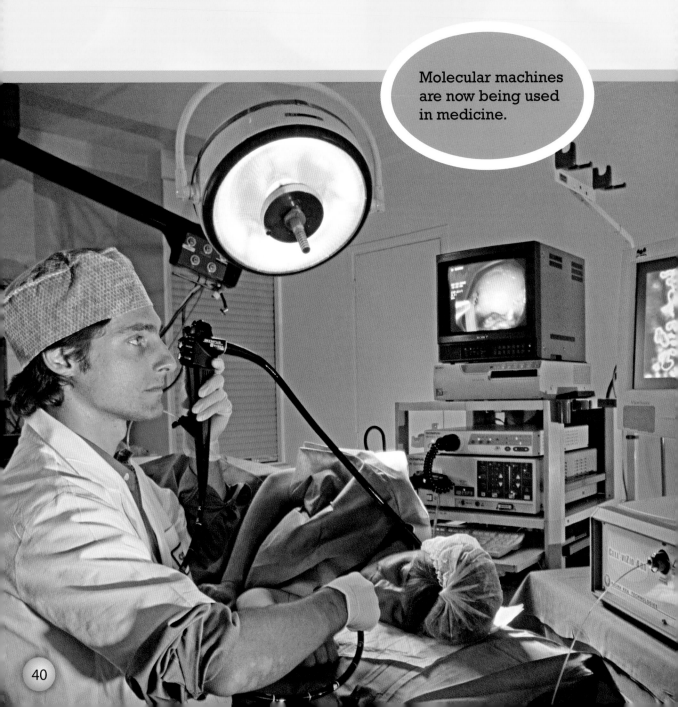

Molecular machines are now being used in medicine.

Using nanotechnology

By using nanotechnology, scientists hope to assemble molecules from atoms. There is even the potential for making molecular machines that would make other molecules. The cells of the human body already do this! But scientists hope to use nanotechnology to make nanorobots that a person could put in a liquid and drink. The nanorobots would be programmed to kill cancer cells or deliver medicine.

Nanotechnology could help us make new materials, including plastics and fuels. It also could help us make extremely fast computers or nanorobots that would clean up polluted water.

Reducing waste, saving resources

Scientists want to program molecular machines to make substances. This means we would not use other valuable resources, and there would be no waste. The machines would use only the exact amounts needed to make a product. For example, the machines could make molecules used to make compounds that we now get from oil, reducing the use of oil. They could also make substances to use for paper, eliminating the need to cut down trees.

Learning and using knowledge about atoms can enhance our lives, make new products, and protect our planet.

Did you know?

Some products already use nanotechnology.

• Scientists have developed sunscreens with nanoparticles that hold the sunscreen chemical. The smaller particles of the sunscreens reduce the whitish look from the cream and protect the skin better.

• Scratch-resistant coatings for car windscreens and spectacles use nanotechnology.

Timeline

465 BCE — Ancient Greek philosopher Democritus proposes that **matter** is made of tiny, uncuttable particles he calls **atoms**.

300 BCE — Another Ancient Greek, Aristotle, states that the four **elements** of fire, water, air, and earth make up all matter.

1661 CE — Englishman Robert Boyle (1637–1691) writes "The Skeptical Chemist", in which he disproves Aristotle's ideas of four elements. Boyle also studies and explains properties of gases.

1789 — Frenchman Antoine Lavoisier (1743–1794) proposes the theory of **oxidation**: that all burning is a combination with oxygen.

1807 — Englishman John Dalton (1766–1844) conceives the atomic theory, saying that all matter is made of various atoms that combine into **molecules**.

1869 — Russian Dmitri Mendeleyev (1834–1907) develops the **periodic table of elements**.

1897	J. J. Thomson discovers the **electron** and wins the Nobel Prize for his discovery.
1898	Scientist Marie Curie (1867–1934), born in Poland and working in France, studies the rays coming from uranium and calls them radioactivity. She also discovers two new elements.
1911	New Zealander Ernest Rutherford (1871–1937) proposes a new model for the structure of atoms.
1918	The **proton** is discovered.
1932	James Chadwick discovers the **neutron** while working in Great Britain.
1939	The first controlled nuclear reaction is achieved by Enrico Fermi, an Italian.
1963	The existence of **quarks** is proposed. Scientists believe that protons and neutrons are made up of quarks.
1977	Scientists find the first evidence of quarks.

Review

◆ Everything in the universe is made of **matter**. Matter has mass and takes up space. Matter can be solid, liquid or gas.

◆ Matter is made up of tiny particles called **atoms**. An atom is the smallest particle of a chemical **element** that still has the properties of that element. An element is a substance made up of all of one kind of atom.

◆ An **electron** is a particle with a negative charge. It is a part of every kind of atom. A **proton** is a particle with a positive charge. Every kind of atom has a different number of protons.

◆ The **nucleus** is the centre of an atom. It contains the protons and **neutrons**. Electrons have a certain amount of energy that keep them floating around the nucleus of an atom. Each atom of an element has equal protons and electrons.

◆ When atoms combine with one another, they form **molecules** and **compounds**. Compounds contain atoms of two or more elements held together by chemical bonds. Molecules are the smallest units formed when atoms combine with each other.

◆ A **chemical reaction** happens when atoms of one element combine with atoms of another element. There are several signs that show a chemical change has occurred. A chemical change is different than physical change. These are both different than a mixture.

◆ Matter changes state because of a change in temperature or pressure.

◆ Something that has a lot of mass in a small space is said to have a high **density**.

Glossary

atom smallest particle of a chemical element that still has the properties of that element. Atoms are considered the "building blocks" of matter.

boiling point temperature at which a substance changes from a liquid to a gas

buoyancy upward force exerted on an object by a fluid

chain reaction continuous reactions caused by one initial reaction

chemical change change of matter's identity and properties, in which old chemical bonds are broken and new chemical bonds are made. Contrasts with a physical change.

chemical reaction see *chemical change*

compound consists of atoms of two or more elements held together by chemical bonds

condense reduce to a more compact or dense form

density measure of mass in a certain volume

diffusion process where particles mix together as a result of movement

electricity flow of electrons through a conductor, such as metal

electron particle outside the nucleus of an atom that has a negative charge

element substance made up of all one kind of atom

energy ability to do work. May take many forms, including light, heat, electricity, sound, or the potential energy of chemical bonds.

lubricant substance that makes movement between solid surfaces slippery

matter "stuff" that makes up everything in the universe

mass amount of matter in something

melting point temperature at which a substance changes from a solid to a liquid

mixture two or more things stirred together that do not react into a new molecule

molecule smallest particle of a substance that still has all the properties of the substance

neutron particle inside the nucleus of an atom that does not have a charge

neutrino extremely tiny particle with no electric charge

nucleus part of an atom that includes the protons and neutrons

orbit curved path of one object around another. Electrons orbit the nucleus.

oxidation chemical reaction in which oxygen combines with a substance, or a reaction in which atoms lose electrons

periodic table of elements A table that lists the known elements, organized according to the element's properties

physical change change where matter is the same, but the form changes

plasma fourth state of matter, not normally found on Earth, that is the result of electrons being stripped from gas atoms

product substance that a chemical reaction produces

proton particle inside the nucleus of an atom that has a positive charge. The number of protons in an atom tells what the atom is.

quark tiny particle that makes up protons and neutrons

radioactivity describes elements that emit high energy rays and particles

synthetic fuel fuel that can be made artificially by chemical reactions

volume amount of space an object or substance takes up

Further information

Books to read

A History of Super Science: Atoms and Elements, Andrew Solway (Raintree, 2006)

Building Blocks of Matter: Elements and Compounds, Louise and Richard Spilsbury (Heinemann Library, 2007)

Chemicals in Action: Atoms, Chris Oxlade (Heinemann Library, 2007)

Chemicals in Action: States of Matter, Chris Oxlade (Heinemann Library, 2007)

Websites

http://www.chem4kids.com
A great site for finding out all about matter, atoms, and more.

http://www.chemsoc.org/viselements
This highly graphic site allows you to visualize the elements and learn more about the periodic table.

http://www.pbs.org/wgbh/aso/tryit/atom/
Build your own atom at this website!

http://www.particleadventure.org
An interactive site, explaining the fundamentals of matter and forces!

Look it up!

Do some more research on one or more of these topics:
• Scanning tunnelling microscope
• Carbon buckyball and geodesic domes

Index